25 Seconds of Horror

"I'm Alright, Dad."

By Stanley Atkins

CHAPTER 1

This is a true story. It was not written in search of pity or sorrow. It was written to let the world know how grateful I am to God for being with me on a dark Chattanooga evening. I have never felt as much horror as I did that night. I suppose it was that way for both of us, but I have to believe it was worse for me because my fourteen year old son, Connor, was traveling with me. He is everything to me, my inspiration and my entire life revolves around him. We instantly became close the second he was born. I remember sitting in a rocker for the first thirty-six hours of his life and refused to let the nurses touch him, unless it was to take his vital signs. I'm not sure what makes him so special and different from any of my other children, but the bond I developed with him was instant. I have another son and three daughters that I love very much. They were older an already and had their own families when Connor was born. I nicknamed him Smurf and still call him that to this day. He was born with a major leg problem and I knew he would never live a normal life like the one I had lived. Perhaps it was the combination of these things that made him so special to me.

The events that occurred on November 23rd, 2013 at 12:30am were beyond my control. I was never prepared to face a time in which I was no longer able to take control of the situation and protect my child. I have a very strong personality and have always been able to face any situation and handle it wisely, or maybe sometimes not so wisely, but you get the point. This was different, though, because I was not in control; however, God was. Have you ever lived in a moment that you will never really understand? The feelings followed by this beat through your heart and they race through your mind. What happens when you can no longer help your child, when the dark of the night takes over and the panic sets in? I could never imagine what was in store for us as. Not knowing the horror that awaited us two and half hours away from our home. Never even thinking or even feeling the coldness that a dark night in the mountains of Tennessee in the month of November brings.

It was the weekend before Thanksgiving. Normally, it's a joyous time for friends and family to gather and prepare to celebrate. They relax, sit around and recount stories from the past or talk about their children. Unfortunately, that was not the case for my son and I. It was not joyful. It was not a happy fun filled time for us. We would not be talking to anyone about any of these things or even thinking about them. Only horror and shock would be felt and the fear of death sets in.

As our families were grocery shopping for the turkey, the stage was being set for tragedy to hit 2 1/2 hours from our home for us. The joyful feeling of Thanksgiving would not be felt for Smurf and I. We would not be sitting around the food filled table, surrounded by family and close friends that bring us all together every year at this time. Instead of thanking God for our family and the food he had given us this joyful day we will be thanking him for something far greater this Thanksgiving.

CHAPTER 2

I will never forget the never ending sounds. The fear and horror that awaited us in the dark of the night, one that is darker than all that we have spent away from our safe, warm home. The sounds replay themselves, fresh in my mind every day as if it is happening all over again.

November 22rd 2013, 10:01 P.M.

Connor and I started out on our much anticipated adventure, leaving the safety of home behind us. It was to be an enjoyable trip out to Missouri for an elk and wild boar hunt. It was going to be his first big game hunt. We were excited, not knowing the horror that awaited us only a couple of hours away. It would change our life forever. It was a horror that one could not handle if God was not there with you. Only God could handle something as sudden and unexpected as this. You have no control over yourself or your child regardless of who you are. Things were going well. Connor was entertaining himself on his phone, playing a game. I was just driving with my thoughts and anticipation. We would talk occasionally about different things. Every so often I would make him get off his phone to talk to me. Our trip set us out from our home to I-85 south where we would travel I-285 westbound, toward I-75 north, toward Chattanooga Tennessee.

As we hit the ramp from I-285 to get on I-75 I was becoming very excited for my son. He loves to hunt and I enjoy doing things for him that make him happy. We passed signs along the road saying this town or that town was ahead so many miles. When we got to Dalton, Georgia I knew we were not far from the Tennessee line. Smurf and I joke with each other a lot. He has a great personality and is a fun kid to be around. I was really enjoying the drive with him.

We were taking it easy, just traveling with the traffic. We weren't in a hurry as I planned the trip timing so we would get to the hunting grounds in the morning which was twelve hours away from home. We still had nine and half hours to go but it made no difference as I love the road and have traveled many miles being a salesman in my younger years. Besides that, I had my son, whom I love dearly, traveling with me. What better company would a man want?

As we got closer to the Tennessee line the signs up ahead read "Knoxville North" and "Nashville West" and I needed to take I-24 West. Connor was laid back with his back against the console and his feet propped up on the dash board, next to his window and had his shoes off. He was still playing his game, a game I'm sure he will never forget.

November 23rd, 12:30am

According to my son, we were doing about 65mph as we were approaching the ramp going toward Nashville. When I turned to the left, heading west, I had taken the curved ramp toward Nashville, Tennessee. There was a guard rail dividing the ramp from I-75 to get on I-24. The guard rail divided the two highways so to merge into one.

I was almost at end of the guard rail still on the ramp that separated I-75 north and I-24 west when a car, seemingly from out of nowhere, was heading right toward us at a high speed. I let out a blood curdling scream and jerked my Ford F-150 to the left as fast and hard as I could. I only had a split second and no more to make the move. If I had not, things would have happened quite differently and ended with us hitting the car head on. I had hit the car on the right front side with my right front, which was Connor's side of the truck. I had avoided a head on collision.

The impact was so hard it spun my truck in a complete one hundred and eighty degree circle and had me heading back South East down an embankment. That's when my truck began to flip over. It was so dark that I couldn't see anything in front of me. I screamed, "Nooooo!" when the first roll began. After about the third roll I yelled, "I'm sorry!" to my son twice. He obviously didn't know why I was apologizing or maybe he couldn't hear me over the loud sounds of glass shattering and metal crumbling. I was apologizing, because at that moment, I was certain that we would never see each other on this earth again. The loud, nerve shattering sounds enveloping us were similar to the crushing of a ball of aluminum foil or a drink can.

I have traveled those Tennessee roads many times and I did not know what exactly we were headed for. These roads were very curvy, with hills and valleys. Some with blasted rock dropping several feet straight down, some had rivers down below, most were steep, some with boulders to help keep the land from sliding. It was perhaps a cliff or a river or maybe a mountain. If so, how steep was the mountain? How deep was the river? Were there boulders down the mountain? I had to idea.

Now remember that it was pitch black outside. I could see nothing. All I could hear was the sounds of the truck crashing and the feel of glass hitting me in the face and arms. I was trying to look at where Smurf was. I could not see him because of the darkness. I was gripping the steering wheel, gripping it so hard my hands were hurting but was not about to let go. If I did let go I would be tumbling around the cab of the truck. At this point I did not know if Smurf was still in the truck or not because the glass was coming from everywhere and I knew there were windows busted out.

Some say the other vehicle that we collided with was traveling around ninety miles per hour when we hit each other. My truck was actually flipping at first because of the speed we were traveling from the impact. At some point we had rolled and flipped more than ten times. Calculating the truck at six feet wide and six feet tall, we had traveled twenty four feet, per roll down a four hundred foot embankment. It could have rolled sixteen times, but at the wreck sight later I only saw marks of the truck hitting the ground that I could see that the rolls and flipping could only be over ten times.

At some point during the incident I was not able to hold onto the steering wheel any longer. My right hand was being pulled from the steering wheel by a force so powerful that I could no longer keep a grip on the wheel. Then my left hand quickly followed and no matter how hard I was trying to hold on it was as if someone was pulling on me. That's the last thing I actually remembered in the truck.

At that point I blacked out. Still today, I have no idea of where I left the truck as all the windows were out except the two on my side, no moon roof, no windshield, no back window and no windows on the passenger side were left. All of those were gone.

God had taken my conscious away from me as he did not want me to see what was to happen next.

God has His ways of talking to you, even though at the time you do not know, you do not listen or you do not even understand and more than often, most of us do not listen.

The next thing I remember is when I woke up on the ground in an awkward position. It was almost as if someone had laid my body down in that spot. I was in a position as if I had been making snow Angels and I was just looking up at the dark sky. As I looked back now, it was more like a movie. Like I was just looking at someone who was supposed to be dead and they had opened their eyes quickly looking straight up. Except that person was me!!! For a split second I did not remember where I was or why I was there. All that I knew was that I had awakened with unbearable pain in my back.

Later I would find out that I had crushed my twelfth vertebrae and cracked the tenth and eleventh. Many ribs were broken and cracked and I had a bruised lung as well.

Then it occurred to me that I had been in a wreck. Out of the corner of my right eye I could see my truck laying upside down slammed next to the tree that had stopped it about fifty feet up the hill from where I was laying. If not for God's intervention with that certain tree and it stopping my truck, the truck would have rolled over me as I was down below.

The motor was sizzling and smoke was coming up all around the front of the truck, where at times you could not even see the front of the truck because of all the smoke. I went crazy. I started to scream, yelling and crying for my son like I had never before. "Smurf! Smurf! Smurf! Where are you, where are you Smurf?!" I tried to get up but could not walk so I looked at my toes and proceeded to try to wiggle them. I was wondering if I was paralyzed. I wasn't. I still could not stand however. Crying my eyes out and still screaming, yelling for Smurf I clinched my nails in the dirt and started to crawl toward the truck. I still had no idea where he was. Was the truck on him? Was he in a tree or maybe below me?

It was incredibly scary for me to think of these possible scenarios. My mind was spinning, it was very dark and I still had no idea where I was or how long I had been unconscious. There was no one around to help. I could hardly see anything except the truck was smoking more and more and making more noise. It was hard for me to think about anything except for my son. Unless you have children and you can't find them in this kind of situation you could never feel this kind of horror. I was ejected out of the truck, so was he as well? I just knew that I had to get to that truck and find him.

Suddenly, it was as though the excruciating pain went away. I was more concerned about finding my son than anything that I was feeling. I was digging as fast as anyone ever could, dragging my feet and legs behind me as if they were useless, all the time with the thoughts of what had happened to my son racing through my mind. At times I could not breathe and had to stop to catch my breath. I felt very exhausted. My screams and crying itself took a lot of strength and air and energy out of me. I had yet to see anyone. No one had come to help us yet. Did anyone even know we were down here? I could hear cars swishing by up the hill side, but still could not see or hear anyone. It was dark and my truck was black but it seems that someone could see the smoke from the motor and wonder what was burning. I could now smell the smoke, it smelled like burning oil.

At some point we've all seen a car exploding in a movie or on TV, but that really never entered my mind at the time. If it had, it still would not have stopped me trying to find my son. My chest began to hurt with every breath I took and every inch I crawled. My hands and fingers were numb at that point. My finger nails were full of dirt. I'm sure my whole under body was as it had rained at some point earlier that day. I couldn't move very fast because every time I yelled out for Connor, it took my breath away.

As I crawled closer to the truck I could hear it sizzling louder and louder. I could see the motor as the smoke was literally rolling out by that time. I had clawed and dragged my way to the truck until I was close enough to see instrument panel lights through the windows lit up. My truck was upside down. There didn't seem to be any smoke inside the cab of the truck. I couldn't tell if the headlights were still on or not, but both the front and rear side windows were still intact on the driver's side.

Later I would find out those were the only two windows left unbroken as the others were totally broken out of the truck. However I could only see the dashboard lit up through the dark glass.

The windshield was shattered and almost completely torn out of the truck. There was a huge hole in it as if someone had gone through it. It looked like a person's body could have possibly gone through it. I wondered if that was where my son had exited the truck.

"Where is my son?" I asked.

I had yet to hear or see Connor at all. I laid there awhile, scared of what I might see. I was crying my eyes out. I was breathless. At that point I was afraid to make another move.

When Connor was raised, he and I spent as much time as possible together. I would do all the boy things with him. When he was a little baby I would take him out in the woods and lay him on a blue blanket as I cut fire wood. He has been through many painful operations since he was 18 months old. I always thought my life would not be a life at all without him.

I laid there a moment, but knew that I still had to get to that truck. I crawled as close as I possibly could and in the middle of a full forced lunge I heard the three most beautiful and heartwarming words any father could ever hear.

"I'm alright, Dad."

Connor seemed to be okay, but he was trapped inside the truck under the steering wheel. He had somehow ended up on the driver's side. I told him to kick the window and he tried, but he couldn't break it. The moon roof was out, but the truck was upside down so that wasn't an option. The windshield could've been an option but there was not much room between the ground and the windshield itself. Besides that, Connor would've had to find something to shield himself with as he crawled through the broken glass. The truck continued to sizzle and smoke as I decided what to do to free my son from the truck.

CHAPTER 3

We set out earlier in the evening to go on a hunting trip and had packed several guns. I looked around, realizing that our guns were scattered everywhere just like everything else from the truck. There was a 9mm Berretta Pistol on the ground beside of me. I quickly picked it up because I saw it as a way to get Connor out of the truck. I told him to stay under the steering wheel because I was going to shoot out the back window. I didn't know if the truck was going to catch on fire or not as it continued sizzling. I'm not sure how long we had been down there because it seemed as if it took forever to drag myself across the ground and to the truck. I still didn't know long I had been unconscious.

I found out later there were hardly any injuries in the other vehicle I had collided with. They also never came down to check on us through whole ordeal. The driver was a nineteen year old with no insurance. How about that? He had three friends with him and seemed as if one of them would have cared enough to see if we were alright.

I could hear traffic passing by us on the road at a high rate of speed. I was about to pull the trigger on the gun when I heard a voice coming from the other side of the truck. A man stuck his head in the broken window on the passage side of the truck and asked Connor if he was alright and if he was the driver or if there was there anyone else in the truck.

I heard Connor reply, "No there isn't and I'm alright. My dad was driving and he is on the other side of the truck, now, down the hill a bit."

The man helped Connor get out of the truck and Connor told him that he would be okay and that he could walk. It only took a second for him to realize that his leg was broken. He began hopping around the truck toward me. I heard him ask the man to check on me.

The man made sure that Connor was okay, then came around the truck to see what kind of condition I was in. The man definitely knew what he was doing and how to approach the situation as he cleared the truck first. I saw the man as he began to walk around the truck towards me. I was laying on my stomach exhausted, but still had the gun in my hand. He identified himself as an off duty Florida State Patrol Trooper. He respectfully asked for my gun and I gave it to him. I never got to shoot the window out as I had planned. He unloaded my gun and gave it back to me. Not sure what that was about, but I assume he gave it back to comfort me. I could tell that he was a seasoned officer, very courteous and professional. He was in his mid 50's. The kind of cop you actually wouldn't mind being pulled over by.

Connor made his way to me and he laid down beside me and we held hands. It was a moment that I will never forget. I realized that my phone was in my hand, but it was covered in blood. I wasn't sure when or how I ended up with it. So, I asked my son and the conversation that followed still baffles me.

Me: *"Where'd you find my phone?"*

Connor: *"In the grass."*

Me: *"The grass?" I exclaimed.*

Connor: *"Yep, I found it where the moon roof had broken completely out."*

Me: *"How'd I get it?"*

Connor: *"I threw it out the windshield to you."*

Me: *"Whose blood is this?" Amazingly, I had no marks or scratches on me.*

Connor: *"It's mine."*

Me: *"And how did you get your phone?"*

Connor: *"I looked for it before I got out."*

Good Lord, leave it up to a teen… Let's get our priorities in order here. Forget the truck possibly catching fire or his own safety. He just had to get his phone. His leg looked like it had blood all over it. He also had his shoes on, so I asked him where he had gotten them, because before the wreck he didn't have them on. He replied that they were lying next to him almost as someone had placed them there. I then thought about when I was calling for him all that time as I was digging my way up the hill and wondered why he hadn't answered before he did. He said he then remembered waking looking up and seeing the lights that shine down onto the floor from the upside down truck. It then came to his mind that he had been a wreck and he thought he was dead. Later, I guess he came out of shock and realized he was alive. He said he could hear me crying for him but could not answer.

He explained the wreck as follows:

"It was like in the movie, Saving Private Ryan, when the RPG hit next to Tom Hanks and it messed up his mind. All he could hear were his men telling him to get out of the fire, but he couldn't move."

I discovered, throughout this whole ordeal, exactly what shock is. Until you have encountered something that has given you shock, you will not understand it correctly or fully. Everyone handles it differently because it hits everyone in different ways. As I remember, at times I would lock my eyes on something and not think of anything. Other times my mind would be racing over what had happened or what could have had happened. Some may think about things in your past life. You go in and out of consciousness. Friends, family and hospital staff may be there and you will interact with them but it is only for second before you leave the conversation with your mind.

While we were lying in the grass together, Connor was apparently trying to call his mother. She was in Atlanta, two hours away at the time, but she would get there as quickly as she could. She could hear the sirens in the background of his call. He later told me that his mother was crying while they were on the phone.

I heard the State Trooper say to Connor, "Hear the sirens? Help is coming."

Ambulances, fire trucks and several Policeman began showing up. The sirens were coming from several directions. During that time I called a friend to come up, but could not get them to answer. I then called another friend. When he answered I told him what happened and to get in touch with my friend, Savannah, because I couldn't get her to answer the phone. He said he was in Atlanta, but I quickly responded that I didn't care where he was or what he was doing. I never ask him for anything and I really needed him to do this. I ended up calling my Policeman friend, who lives up the road. I knew he could help. He called a county deputy and they went to wake my friend, Savannah, up. She eventually awakened after they beat on several doors and windows. I then proceeded to call my friend Rick, and told him to pick up Savannah and get up here immediately as I needed her. I knew she would take of us. I was calling several friends as I was lying on my back in the grass at the wreck sight. In the weeks following, I would find out one by one because I had no memory of it.

There were several EMT there and two ambulances that was there. Several were working on Connor and three were working on me. While I was talking on the phone the female EMT would take my phone away and when someone else passed by I would ask them to give it back to me. This happened several times before they loaded me up. They had also put a head and neck brace on me and cut off my clothes before they loaded me in the ambulance.

CHAPTER 4

I was in so much pain I did not want anyone to touch me,
but I knew they had to. So two men put me on the gurney
and when they did they slipped on the damp grass and
dumped me off the gurney. I was not a happy camper at
this point and was far from being nice after that.

The first officer on the scene was not much of a talker as I
didn't remember him saying anything. He wore glasses and
was a heavy set man, completely different from the second
officer who was young. He was a rookie for sure. He was
more interested in categorizing the scene as a drug deal
gone wrong. I believe that was more important to him than
our well-being. I can imagine him thinking, "Now, let us
get a confession out of these people before they die!"

He shined his flash light all around and then on my face
asking, "What is all this money for? And why do you have
so many guns?"

When I travel a far distance I put my money in my cup
holder because I do not want it in my back pocket. It's an
uncomfortable way to travel. That answered that question
for him and as many times that the truck rolled over, almost
everything was thrown out of it. I explained that we were
going on a hunting trip and that was why we had so many
guns. My hunting agreement was in the truck or somewhere
around there, if he would've actually look for it. He acted
as if he hardly believed me. I guess it could have looked
like a drug deal as there was money, assault rifles, and
pistols scattered and lots of bullets and clips. We were

going to have fun shooting once we got there. I had several coolers in the back to pack the meat of whatever we killed in, which were scattered all around, too. That may have been a flag for him to think this as a gone wrong drug deal as he thought the coolers were to pack illegal drugs or marijuana.

I remember them questioning my son about where we were going and how fast were we driving. He replied about the hunt and told them that were going about 65 or so. I also heard someone ask my son how old he was and they then decided that he would go to the children's ward in the same hospital I was headed for. Later Connor told me that there was another boy who was already in the ambulance. He apparently was picked up from another incident and they came to get Connor as well before heading to the hospital. As the wreck had been reported over the radio to the EMC and police how bad it was. Anyway, do you think we were charged half of an ambulance bill? Of course not, his bill was the same as mine: $1,240.00

When they finally got me in the ambulance a female EMT stayed in the back with me. I had a very hard time breathing and would complain about it with every breath, but she wouldn't do anything or say anything. At the time I was not aware that I had several broken and cracked ribs and that was why I could hardly breathe. The EMT warned me that she was about to stick me. I told her that didn't bother me as I donate blood to Red Cross every two weeks, so that was the least of my worries. What I really needed was a breathing machine. She told me to slow down and take long deep breaths. All I could think about was my son and how he was doing. I would go in and out of conscious on the way to the hospital, never remembering much. They took me to the ER trauma area. I did actually remember being transferred from the ambulance bed to another bed and again I did not want to be touched. Every time they did, I went crazy. The pain was unbearable. Several nurses were all around me doing what they do, poking me with needles and pumping me full of whatever they pump hurt people with. Finally I was put on a breathing machine. Then I was left alone hurting and continuing to call numerous people. I did not remember who all I called until they also told me several weeks later. Funny thing though, apparently I called Erick, at Akin Ford to order a new truck for myself at six thirty in the morning. He took the call and told me about it later on because I had no recollection of attempting to order a new truck. Now, that's what I call customer service!

The hurt seemed to fade away eventually as the meds were kicking in. I made another phone call to someone and they were asking me which hospital I was in. I realized that I didn't even know. A male nurse was close by so I told him to take my phone and tell these people where I was. He refused stating that there was blood on my phone and he was not going to touch it. We settled by putting my phone on speaker so he could name the hospital.

I over heard someone say that no one could come in the Trauma Center unless they were immediate family. I quickly called Rick and Savannah before they arrived to tell them to claim themselves as my brother and daughter. That is how I came to have my operation.

While I was laying in the ER my lips were ridiculously dry and chapped. I politely asked a nurse if she had anything I could put on them. She gave me a tube on some minty chap stick. It felt very good. Later I ask her for more and she refused to give me anymore. As she left there was a janitor in the room cleaning I asked if he could give it to me because it was not in my reach. He did not speak English and I knew he was not Hispanic as I have been to thirty-three different countries in my life, but I still said "uno por favor, el momento" and held the one up I had and pointed to the direction of the others out of my reach. The nurse came in later and asked where I had gotten it from. I was told later that I was in the trauma ER for around thirty hours. Time was going by fast, so I figured that I was sleeping through most of it.

I do recall Rick and Savannah walking in. They both had big smiles on their faces. Later, I was told that my sister, Pandora, was the first one in the ER, but I did not remember that. She was told she had to step outside because of hospital policies about how many visitors were allowed at a time. I wasn't sure what day it was or what time of day it was. Two nurses came into move me into yet another bed. Instead of musical chairs they play musical beds. They must like to apply pain on folks for the yelling music they create. They picked the sheet up underneath me and just switched me over. Boy, do I remember this because it was mighty painful. After this I was no longer nice to them, either, as I was told. I mean, when someone hurts you what are you supposed to do, thank them?

After moving beds I was in a normal room. I would be woken up from time to time as different friends and family members were coming and going. I remember my older son, Ronnie, and his sister were there as someone woke me up and said your son, Ronnie is here. I remember he was on my right side with a big smile and said something and his sister, Stephanie was on my left and also said something. They had a little girl with them as well. Ronnie said he had stayed for a while and helped the doctor fit me in my body brace which I had no recollection of. All I remember is that someone woke me up and me seeing his smiling face. That's all I remember about my older son being there. My friends came down from Athens and Tennessee to visit. Pandora had put her vacation on hold and came to see me twice. The second time she brought her husband with her. I have never called him by name because it reminds me of a candy bar I don't like. His name is Kit. My sister told me later on, that when they entered the room I called him by name and they each looked at each other and said that they may themselves have to go to the ER because they were in shock. Shock and meds mixed makes you do weird things. Even though I look back and see a majority of horror, there were many funny things that happened as well.

The doctor wanted to operate and I would not let him. I told him, "Take me to Athens to get operated on." As if I even knew anyone could even do the operation there. It was then declared that I was not even capable of making the decision myself. So, he stated that my so-called "daughter", Savannah, and my sister Pandora would make the decision for me. Savannah immediately said yes because my sister had already left to resume her vacation. They knew what was best for me. Someone said that I needed an MRI and they asked if I was claustrophobic. At that point I yelled, "Do not put me in that tube!"

"Well that's the answer to that question." The doctor smirked. So, they sedated me and did it anyway. Later my sister found out that this hospital was one of the best in the country for that type of operation.

Me & Connor a few years ago.

This is Exit 2 toward Chattanooga & Nashville, Tennessee.
At this point our destiny was sealed. It's the last exit sign
we saw before the accident. Our lives would quickly be
changed forever; the talks, the laughter and comradery of
our hunting trip would soon come to an end.

Erlanger Emergency Room. I was taken there by
Ambulance after the accident.

Erlanger Children's Hospital where my son was able to stay and be cared for while I was in the adult Erlanger center.

Erlanger Children's Hospital.

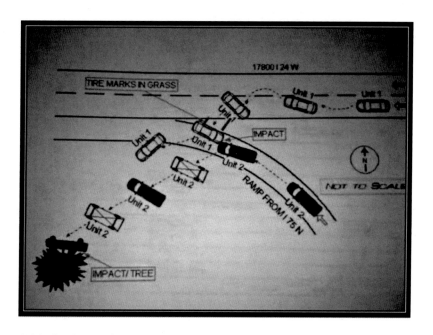

This is the accident report that was drawn up by the police. My truck is shown as on its side, laying against a tree. It was actually completely upside down, laying on its top. We rolled at least ten times although the report only shows twice.

This is my truck after the accident. As you can see, it's a miracle that we both survived.

"I'm alright, Dad." Those are the first words that I heard from my son when I feared the worst after the accident. Once I was out of the hospital I had t-shirts made up with his quote and the date of the accident.

CHAPTER 5

Many of the things in this story that happened after the wreck were recounted to me in the weeks that followed. Apparently, when you are in shock and on medication it messes with your head and memory.

During the whole stay at every waking moment I was always concerned about Smurf. That's all I could think about. I still wasn't sure how bad he was hurt and no one had told me. I had yet to see him because he was in a completely different part of the hospital. He is a very strong boy but till this day he still has no idea of the magnitude of this wreck. So horrible and so devastating that the wrecker man that went to get the upside down truck but could not use the one he drove there. They had to call another wrecker to help get it and the wrecker man whom pulled it in had told some friends of mine that had went to the yard where the truck had been stored, that he has been in this business for forty-nine years and never seen anyone walk away from a wreck such as this one. Connor has had so many painful operations. He simply brushed it off as a mere fender bender or a playful four wheeler wreck, as he often does.

Connor's stay lasted two nights for observation. He told me later on that he had heard things falling in his hospital room. He said that he asked his mom what it was and she said that it was nothing. He also said he had nightmares while he was there. After the two night stay his mom checked him out and a nurse wheeled him over to see me in a wheel chair, then they headed home to Jefferson. Connor told me later that on the way home he was scared of each bump or move the car had taken during the trip. His mom hired a private ambulance plane to take him to the hospital in West Palm Beach, Florida to his regular leg doctor. He had to get there quickly and could not fly on a commercial airline because he could not bend his knee and time was important. Connor had told me at a later date that he did not know we were in a wreck until the first roll started and he heard the metal crushing and then he said he started rolling around in the truck and remembered being slammed up what he felt was like a wall and that was the last thing he remembered at that point he had blacked out. He said he also remembered me yelling out a scream and thought that may have been the one he heard before we hit.

In the weeks following, Danny Otter transferred me back to our home. For about the first four weeks I was on a breathing machine because of the damage done. I also wore a body brace that I still wear till this day. Connor came home to be with me. I could not keep my eyes off him and did not want to miss anything his voice said. I had already moved from my bed room to the living room sofa and he stayed on the other one for weeks. I spent every waking second with my son. I work my time around his school and his things he has to do in his life even though my businesses may suffer because I do these things for him. Someone who knows me well said to me. "Stan, you would be happy in life if you only had a nickel in your pocket and had your son." Now, I spend even more time with him and focus on raising him to be a better boy and try to teach him to be a man and be able to learn to take care of himself and his future family. When something like this happens it certainly changes your priorities in life. Don't wait for something like this for you to change yours. After a few weeks went by someone had brought me a box of things from my truck and I told them I had no intentions of even wanting to see them, but Connor did. I was standing in the kitchen and Connor walked in with my Bible that I always kept in my truck.

He said, "Dad, here's why were still alive." I choked up.

I got control of my emotions and in a squatting position and said, "Yes, it is, son."

God and his Angels were there with us. My Bible was totally intact. Over the years I have kept personal things in it that were dear to me. Nothing, not a thing had been moved, not even a piece of glass was in it like everything else that flew out of the truck.

A month or so after I drove back up to Chattanooga to get my belongings from the Police Department. As they keep your guns for a while to run background checks and also to see if the guns were registered. I went back to the wreck sight and calculated the time of impact to the time the truck landed beside the tree and it was less than twenty-five seconds. That's the reason I have called this story *"25 Seconds of Horror."*

The first day I went back to my store I walked up to my office, went to grab the door knob but I hesitated a second and said to myself, "I'm not supposed to be here."

I had ordered a new truck just like the one I was driving when the wreck happened. I will not drive anything else. God sure taught Ford how to build a safe truck. It had the most air bags I have ever seen in a vehicle. The entire truck held up throughout the entire wreck. When my new truck finally came in a few months later it took me two weeks to get up the nerve to go get it. As I was walking to look at the truck a scary feeling hung over me. When I finally went to see it I was afraid to open the door and procrastinated doing so. Finally when I got the strength to do so, my eyes went directly to the console right up to the right front dash board where my son was positioned when we wrecked. I actually visualized him there. A strong feeling went over me as if we were still on the trip. It was not the wreck I was feeling, it was the trip itself that I saw in my mind, as if it was just a dream that never even happened, but it was not a dream! I immediately closed the door and went inside to sign the papers. I then went and got me a coke, stood around for bit until I collected my emotions to get in the truck. The coke was still completely full the next day in the cup holder in my truck. I never took a sip. My mind was confused about life itself.

Our life on this earth can be taken like a flicker of a flame. We never know when it is our time. Just be ready and be right with God. Don't wait for something like this to happen to set you straight. No doubt, doing things that you know is wrong in God's sight are fun sometimes but you will pay for them one day. It is like smoking or eating fried foods, they taste good but are bad for you. I not saying for you to stop either, it's just an example of what I'm trying to say to you. Watch who you hang with and call your friends and what you do with them. A real friend will not guide you in the wrong direction. If you know it is wrong they are not your friends. Remember when you are in front of God one day your so called friends won't be with you. It is your choice what roads to take in life and what signs you see and use. Don't think running a stop sign won't hurt someone. It will and you will pay for it. You will have to repair it or repair who you hurt.

Roads in life get bumpy sometimes. You will have curves and hills and mountains and valleys to deal with and sometimes it is hard to steer in the right direction, but again it is your choice and no one else's. It may be God testing you to make you strong or to use you one day to help others. If you have children when you run the stop sign then you will have to one day deal or they will have to deal with their consequences. Stop teaching them bad things. I know drinking that one margarita and getting under the steering wheel is not teaching them the right thing to do. Children will automatically do what you do. You must learn stop at lights and don't get impatient. God will tell you when to go. When one of your so called friends is the driver and goes and does bad things that you know quite well is wrong, get yourself another driver. In the end it will be you that has to live with what choice you made. If God wants to change you, He will. Don't wait till something like this wreck has to change you. This wreck has changed my life in a positive way and making me a better person and I'm trying to raise my son in a better way.

The change will not be over night. He has already taken the taste of beer and any kind of alcohol away from me. It is one of the best things lately that has happened to me. I love life more. I drink mostly Raspberry Ginger Ale, now. He has already saved me a lot of money and it keeps me from acting up the way that I do when I drink alcohol.

There is a God, I know, because He was there that night with us. God and His Angels.

When I was leaving the truck that night, it was God pulling me out. He held me then dropped me and told me it was going to hurt me, but not too much. Imagine this… how could my lifeless body fly through the air, traveling some height and speed, yet I only suffered minor injuries compared to what it should or could have been? I was laying on the ground as if someone had placed me there. There were no other limbs broken, no scratches and no neck injuries. There is only one answer.

God said to me that He wanted me to live because my son still needs me. I need to raise him right because he will be a great man one day and God knows that.

God said, "I had two of my Angel's hold Connor in the truck so he would be safe as I know you could never live without him. He needs you and you need him. I have plans for you both. Now, suffer with your pain and every time you feel it, remember me. Ask me every day what you can do for me and listen when I answer. I will guide you and your son in the right direction."

CHAPTER 6

Any of you can look at this story and easily pick things out of it to prove God is present. If He wasn't then we wouldn't be alive right now. Maybe, just maybe, God allowed the wreck to change our lives for the better and for us one day to do work for him.

I ask God every morning, during the day and when I lay down at night. "What do *You* want me to do for *You?*" I have not gotten an answer yet. I have no idea and no one else does, only He does and it will be shown to me on His time, not mine. Maybe I was suppose writing about this accident and maybe this story has touched someone.

When He is ready He will show me.

And as I'm sure you've been wondering, Connor escaped only with a hairline fracture below his knee, a cut knee, two broken ribs and a slight concussion.

There are two major things that after all this time that come to my mind. One is the first roll and the other is when I saw my truck upside down and did not know where my son was. Sometimes is seems as if I'm living it all over. Time will go by and I know this will one day not be so prevalent in my mind.

I want to thank all my friends and family members that helped Connor and me through all this. Many of you took time out of your lives and from your work and your own family life to help us. There were most that I did not even remember helping. I had found out this over the next few months.

I want to recognize my friends at the Double Tree Hotel in West Palm Beach for all their support, prayers, and gifts they provided for Smurf and their kindness concerning the accident. The hotel was home during his four month stay. During his major leg operations they actually became more of a family and were very kind to my son and made his stay comforting. At times we were able to come back to our farm in Nicholson and when we returned to West Palm they would meet him with his favorite milk shake (and they don't even serve or offer them). They also had his name on the marquis. Everyone would come out to welcome him back and into his room. They had welcome back balloons and his favorite snacks and drinks. They totally went over board to comfort him and I am truly grateful for this.

I thank my sister Pandora and her family for taking time out of their vacation to help take care of me. Anthony Porter and others such as Sherry Miller spent time at my house a few days that I had no recollection of to help with me. My son, Ronnie, that had spent time with me in the hospital with which I only remember seeing him one time when he first got there. They were many people who visited me, brought food, sat with me and helped others with me, there where to many to count, many at the times I do not even remember they were even around me. My best friends, Gomer and Temberly, from Athens, Tennessee came down to see me. But there is one girl, Savannah, that quit her job, came to Chattanooga, Tennessee and stayed with me the whole time and stayed with Connor and I all the time when we came home and took care of us. Connor and I thank you from the depth of our hearts. We are more than grateful to you Savannah.

To end this story I would just like to clarify that God is great. He was there with us that night and is with us every day. I have no regrets and no complaints about the wreck. I am only thankful about it.

Life is short, so we should always remember to tell our loved ones how we feel about them. When my son was in middle school I would take him lunch every day. Day after day he would just grab it, tell me thanks and walk away. It wasn't cool for him to show his dad affection in front of his friends any more. One day I stopped him and said, "Son, one day I might walk out that door and it could be the last time you see me alive. You would always regret not giving me a hug and telling me that you loved me." After that he made sure that he always gave me a hug and told me that he loved me.

I do regret many things I have done in my life to hurt people, doing many wrong things. I said things to my own children that I should not have said. I did not spend much quality time with my older children. I thought giving them nice things was the right thing to do. I did not do the right thing with my older son, Ronnie. I said things to my own parents that I should not have said. Over my life time I have done many things I was not supposed to be doing.

All these things haunt me every day of my life. I will see things or do things or hear people say or do things that bring back the hurt I have caused. Sometimes my own children bring back those memories for me. We laugh, we play, we drink and we live every day to cover the scars. There are some that will just never go away.

I was raised up in a simple country life with a good mom and family life. We were poor but my Mom made the best of things. And what did I do? I went out, complicated it and messed it up. I can only hope you do not do the same. Never forget who put you on this beautiful earth and what He can do for **you**.

One last thing….

When I die, on my head stone it will read:

"I'm Alright Son."

Made in United States
Orlando, FL
03 October 2024

52306147R00027